The Science of Insects

LIVING SCIENCE

Janice Parker

Gareth Stevens Publishing
MILWAUKEE

For a free color catalog describing Gareth Stevens' list of high-quality books and multimedia programs, call 1-800-542-2595 (USA) or 1-800-461-9120 (Canada). Gareth Stevens Publishing's Fax: (414) 225-0377.

Library of Congress Cataloging-in-Publication Data

Parker, Janice.
    The science of insects / by Janice Parker.
        p. cm. — (Living science)
    Includes index.
    Summary: Discusses the life cycles, classification, behavior, and habitats of insects.
    ISBN 0-8368-2466-0 (lib. bdg.)
    1. Insects—Juvenile literature. [1. Insects.] I. Title. II. Series: Living science (Milwaukee, Wis.)
    QL467.2.P3425 1999
    595.7—dc21   99-26933

This edition first published in 1999 by
Gareth Stevens Publishing
1555 North RiverCenter Drive, Suite 201
Milwaukee, WI 53212 USA

Project Co-ordinator: Samantha McCrory
Series Editor: Leslie Strudwick
Copy Editor: Ann Sullivan
Design: Warren Clark
Cover Design: Carole Knox
Layout: Lucinda Cage
Gareth Stevens Editor: Patricia Lantier-Sampon

Every reasonable effort has been made to trace ownership and to obtain permission to reprint copyright material. The publishers would be pleased to have any errors or omissions brought to their attention so that they may be corrected in subsequent printings.

Photograph Credits:
Corel Corporation: cover (center), pages 5 top, 5 bottom, 6 bottom left, 7, 8, 9, 11 top, 12, 13, 14, 15 top, 17, 24, 25 top, 25 far right, 25 bottom right, 25 far left, 28; John Fowler: pages 4, 10, 15 bottom, 20, 21 far right, 27 top; Todd Reichardt: page 25 bottom left; Tom Stack & Associates: cover (background) (Jeff Foott), pages 5 far right (Rod Planck), 16 (John Shaw), 18 (Rod Planck), 19 top (David M. Dennis), 19 bottom (David M. Dennis), 21 top (John Shaw), 21 bottom (David M. Dennis), 27 bottom (David M. Dennis), 29 (W. Perry Conway), 31 (David M. Dennis); J.D. Taylor: page 22; Visuals Unlimited: pages 6 top (Bill Beatty), 6 bottom right (William J. Weber), 11 bottom (Richard Thom), 23 (David G. Campbell), 30 (Ken Lucas); Joyce Wang: page 26.

Printed in Canada

1 2 3 4 5 6 7 8 9 03 02 01 00 99

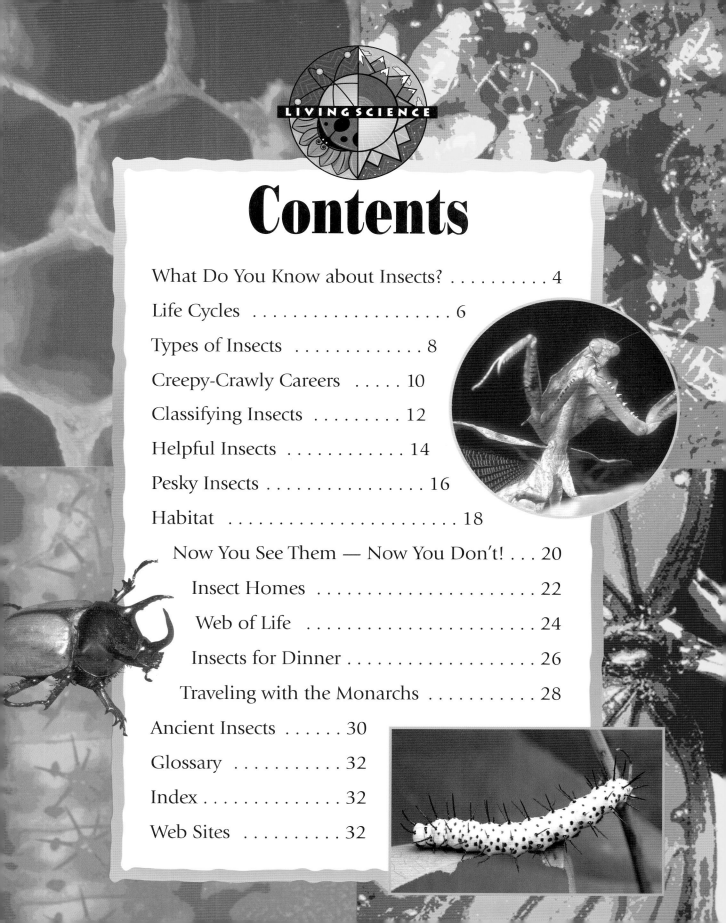

Contents

What Do You Know about Insects?

Insects are a large group of animals that do not have a spinal column, or backbone. Many other groups of animals exist, such as birds, mammals, and reptiles. Insects can be larger than your hand or so small you cannot see them. For every person in the world, there are 200 million insects. All insects have six legs and a body divided into three parts. The outside of their bodies is covered by a hard skeleton called an **exoskeleton**.

More than one million **species** of insects exist in the world.

Puzzler

Spiders are not insects. Do you know why? (Hint: Count their legs!)

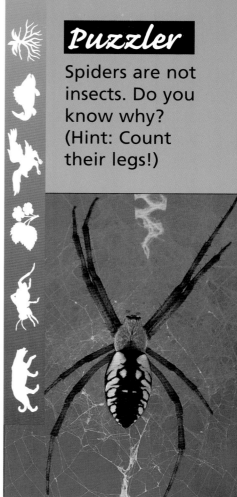

Answer:
All insects have six legs — spiders have eight legs. Spiders are part of a group of animals called **arachnids**. Arachnids are relatives of insects.

Life Cycles

All animals have a life cycle. A life cycle includes a beginning, growth, **reproduction**, and death. Insects, like other animals, follow this life cycle.

Grasshoppers begin their lives as eggs buried in the ground. When an **egg** hatches, a **nymph** comes out. A nymph looks like a small adult without wings. Nymphs shed their skin several times as they grow. This is called **molting**. The grasshopper completes its life cycle when it becomes an adult. Adult grasshoppers have wings and can produce eggs.

Insects have different types of life cycles. Very simple insects hatch out of their eggs looking just like small adult insects. These insects grow larger throughout their lives, but they always look the same. Other insects look quite different at different stages of their life cycle.

Activity

Draw a Life Cycle
Draw a diagram of the life cycle of a colorful butterfly.

Some insects, such as butterflies and beetles, have four parts to their life cycle: egg, **larva**, **pupa,** and adult. Most of these insects begin their lives as eggs. The eggs hatch into larvae, which do not look like the adult insect. Like nymphs, larvae grow larger through molting. During the final molt, the larva surrounds itself in a cover. This is the pupa stage. The pupa in butterflies is called a **chrysalis**. The insect transforms into its adult shape and breaks out of the chrysalis. Adult insects are able to reproduce.

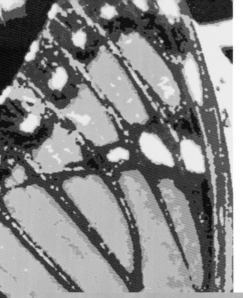

Types of Insects

There are many types of insects, and each one has features that make it different from others. Can you tell the difference between insects?

Types

Crickets and Grasshoppers	Leaf Insects and Stick Insects	Damselflies and Dragonflies	Termites	Cockroaches

Features

• can jump long distances • have two pairs of wings • sing or chirp to communicate with other similar insects	• eat plants • look like sticks or leaves and can easily **camouflage** themselves in their **habitat**	• are excellent flyers • hunt at night	• build nests in logs or on the ground • have two sets of wings • live in large groups	• are flat with long antennae • will eat almost anything

Puzzler

What type of insect is a ladybug?

Answer:
Ladybugs are beetles that have two pairs of wings. The outer pair is the hard, colorful covering of the ladybug.

Praying Mantises	Beetles	Ants, Bees, and Wasps	Butterflies and Moths	Flies and Mosquitoes
• attack and eat other insects • have strong front legs	• have two pairs of wings • include fireflies • one set of wings covers the body in a hard shell	• live in large groups • usually have two pairs of wings	• have two pairs of wings • most butterflies fly during the day • moths usually fly at night	• have one set of wings • flies are one of the fastest flying insects

Creepy-Crawly Careers

Many people work with bugs. People who study bugs are called **entomologists**. To become an entomologist, you must go to a university and study for a degree in science. Many different jobs involve insects. Some entomologists help farmers deal with insects that kill their crops. Others work to prevent diseases that are spread by insects. Some entomologists can even help police solve crimes by looking at insects at crime scenes!

Entomologists use nets to capture insects for study.

Grasshoppers cause damage to wheat crops.

Activity

Do Your Own Research

Many careers involve insects in some way. Find out more about the different types of entomologists. Some of the types of work they do include the following:

- Work with farmers to show how insects can keep their plants healthy
- Study how insects spread disease
- Find out how many insects live in an area
- Teach at universities

Monarch butterflies are tagged for **migration** research.

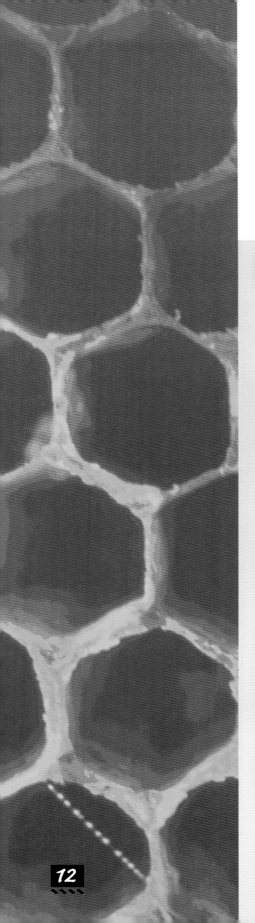

Classifying Insects

Scientists **classify** the many different types of insects into groups. Insects within each group share similar features or behave the same way.

Eyes

compound eyes,
no eyes,
simple eyes

Legs

attacking legs,
digging legs,
jumping legs,
swimming legs

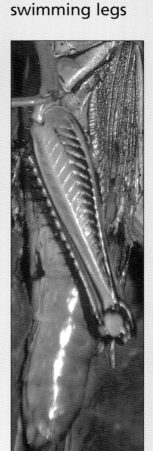

Antennae

beaded,
clubbed,
comblike,
feathery,
sawlike

Activity

Drawing Insects

Think of insects that you have seen or heard about. Draw and color some of them. Group together, or classify, the insects that are similar.

Mouthparts	Habitat	Color	Defense
chewing mouthparts, piercing mouth-parts, sucking mouthparts, tunneling mouthparts	desert areas, people's houses, trees, underground, water	black, blue, brown, red, yellow, gray, other colors	bad smells, bites, scary appearance, spines, stingers

   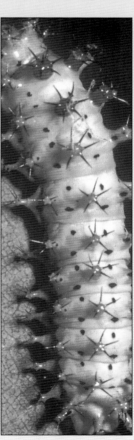

Helpful Insects

Some people dislike all insects, even helpful ones. Many insects are helpful to us. Bees make honey for us to eat. Dragonflies eat mosquitoes. Ladybugs make a meal out of insects that destroy our garden plants. Insects **pollinate** plants. Without insects, we would not have many flowers.

Ladybugs and dragonflies are helpful insects to have in a garden.

Some insects are admired for their beauty. Butterflies can be many brilliant colors. Many of us like the sounds of crickets and grasshoppers. Insects also help keep our neighborhoods clean. When an animal dies or garbage is left outside, insects often eat the remains. If left to rot, these remains could make us or our pets sick.

Silkworms are not worms at all. They are a type of caterpillar. Silkworms spin their cocoons out of a very strong **fiber**. We use this fiber to make a beautiful cloth called silk.

Activity

Use Your Five Senses to Explore Insects

You can learn about the world around you by using all of your five senses.

Listen to grasshoppers or crickets "talking" to one another. Watch a butterfly or moth flying past. Feel the sting of a mosquito. Taste and smell honey made by bees.

1. Spend some time outdoors using your five senses to learn about insects.
2. Write down the names of all the insects you see, hear, or feel.
3. Paint a picture of each insect.
4. Write down which sense or senses you used to learn about each insect.
5. Taste some honey. We could not have honey without the help of bees.
6. Think about your sense of smell. Can you think of any insects that can smell?

Pesky Insects

Many people are scared of insects and their relatives, such as spiders. Most insects are harmless. Even bees and wasps are dangerous only to people with allergies to their stings. Mosquitoes can carry dangerous diseases. In some regions, mosquitoes can spread a disease called malaria. Up to 500 million people get malaria every year. Malaria can kill unless the proper medicine is used.

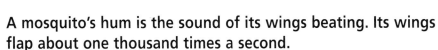

A mosquito's hum is the sound of its wings beating. Its wings flap about one thousand times a second.

Many insects can be annoying. We call these insects pests. Mosquito bites can itch for days. Bee and wasp stings can be very painful. Cockroaches appear in our homes and spread dirt. They will eat almost anything in the house, including shoes. Insect pests can destroy plants and crops. Certain insects like to eat the same plants that humans like to eat. They will even eat the beautiful flowers in our gardens.

Cockroaches, grasshoppers, and bees are sometimes considered pests.

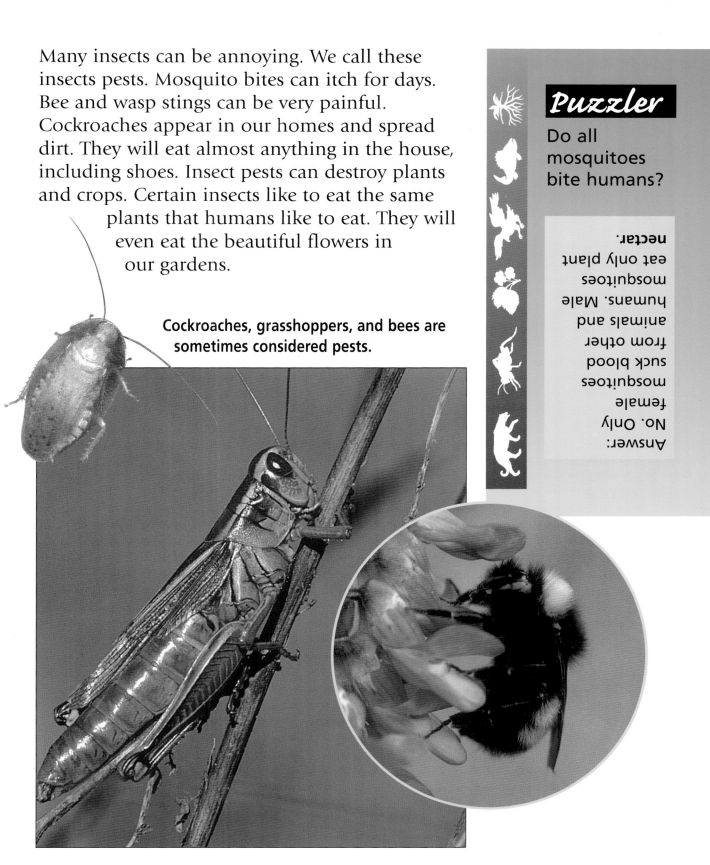

Puzzler

Do all mosquitoes bite humans?

Answer: No. Only female mosquitoes suck blood from other animals and humans. Male mosquitoes eat only plant nectar.

Habitat

An insect's habitat is the area in which it lives. Insects live all around the world. They live in very hot and very cold areas. Insects live in water, underground, in people's homes, and even on other animals. Each type of insect has special features that help it **adapt** to its environment.

Desert Habitats

Insects that live in hot deserts must live in high temperatures with little water. Desert insects avoid the heat by coming out only at night. During the day, they stay underground or beneath rocks. Desert insects are often covered in a thick, waxy coating. This keeps insects from drying out and dying.

Lake and Pond Habitats

Many insects have adapted to living on or in water. The water scavenger beetle swims under the water. The beetle must return to the top of the water to breathe from air bubbles. Water strider insects are able to walk on top of water. Their legs have adapted so that they do not sink into the water.

Roommates for People

Many insects live in houses and buildings with people. Houses provide some insects with a warm place to live all year round. Cockroaches live in many houses. Flour beetles live in dried food goods, such as flour or nuts. Fleas make a home in the skin and fur of dogs and cats.

Now You See Them — Now You Don't!

Insects are food for a number of animals. Many insects avoid being eaten by blending into or disappearing into their habitat. This is called camouflage. A well-camouflaged insect is difficult to see. Moths that are gray and spotted often sit on tree bark during the day. These moths are very hard to see unless they move.

Some insects look just like leaves or other parts of trees. Walking stick insects look just like green or brown sticks on a tree. If a walking stick senses danger, it folds up its legs and falls to the ground like a dead twig. Katydids have wings that look like leaves. When they stop moving, it is difficult to see them on a tree. Most praying mantises are green and look like tree branches. The Kanchong praying mantis is bright pink — just like the flowers on the trees on which it sits.

Certain insects disguise themselves by looking like other animals. These insects are called copycats. Animals avoid hover flies because they look like stinging wasps. Birds will not eat harmless viceroy butterflies. Viceroy butterflies look the same as monarch butterflies, which are poisonous.

Many insects are easy to see but are protected by their hard outer skin. Some caterpillars have sharp spines on their backs. Other animals will often drop these insects when they feel the sharp spikes. Bees and wasps will sting if they are attacked.

Activity

Find the Hidden Insects

Spend some time outside looking for insects. Look for insects that are easy to see and those that are not. Remember to look under leaves and on tree bark. If you see a rock on the ground, turn it over to see if any insects are moving around underneath.

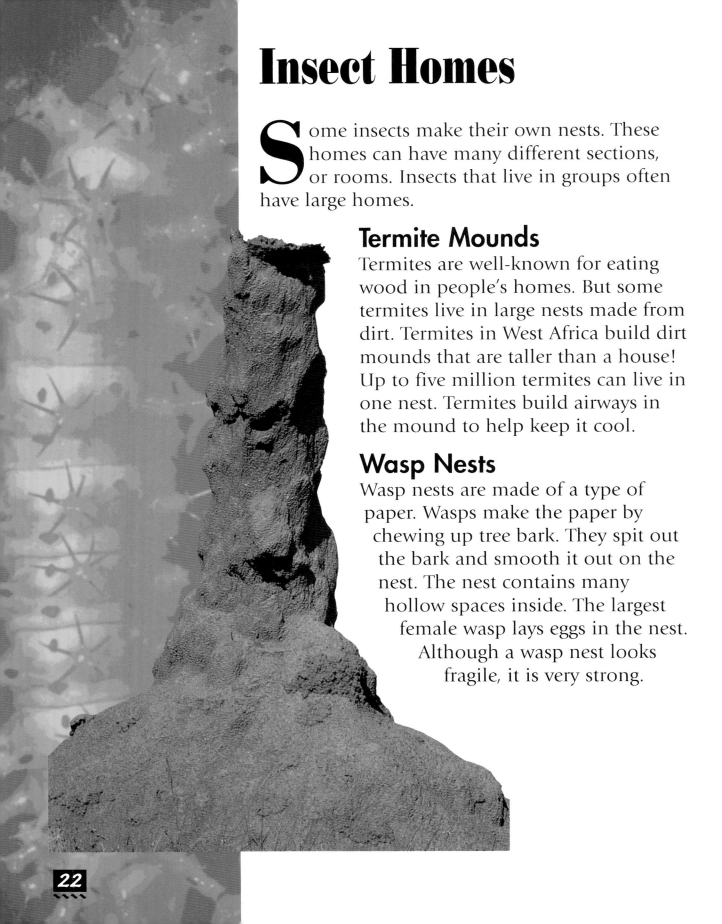

Insect Homes

Some insects make their own nests. These homes can have many different sections, or rooms. Insects that live in groups often have large homes.

Termite Mounds

Termites are well-known for eating wood in people's homes. But some termites live in large nests made from dirt. Termites in West Africa build dirt mounds that are taller than a house! Up to five million termites can live in one nest. Termites build airways in the mound to help keep it cool.

Wasp Nests

Wasp nests are made of a type of paper. Wasps make the paper by chewing up tree bark. They spit out the bark and smooth it out on the nest. The nest contains many hollow spaces inside. The largest female wasp lays eggs in the nest. Although a wasp nest looks fragile, it is very strong.

Ant Farms

South American leaf-cutter ants live underground. They dig out large areas, or rooms. In one room, the queen ant lays eggs. In the other rooms, the ants farm their own food. The ants cut pieces from leaves and flowers and bring them to their underground nest. The plant pieces are placed in the dirt. The ants do not eat the plants. They eat the fungus that grows on the dying plants.

Egg Pots

A potter wasp builds small pots out of mud. It lays an egg in each pot. A wasp also catches a caterpillar to put into each pot. When the eggs hatch, the larvae eat the caterpillar.

Beehives

Bees live in hives. These homes are divided into many sections called honeycomb. Worker bees build honeycomb from wax that they make. The honeycomb holds all the honey needed to feed young bees. Other areas in the hive are used for eggs.

Puzzler

Honey tastes different depending on the beehive. Can you guess why?

Answer: The taste of honey depends on the plants from which the bees gather nectar. Bees that live in different places will make honey that tastes like the plants in that area.

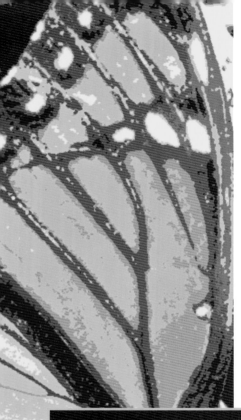

Web of Life

All living things depend on other living things to survive. Each plant and animal plays an important role in its environment. When left undisturbed by humans, plants and animals, including insects, help keep the environment in balance.

Food chains show how plants and animals survive by eating other plants or animals. Energy is transferred from one living thing to another in a food chain. A food web is many food chains that are connected to one another.

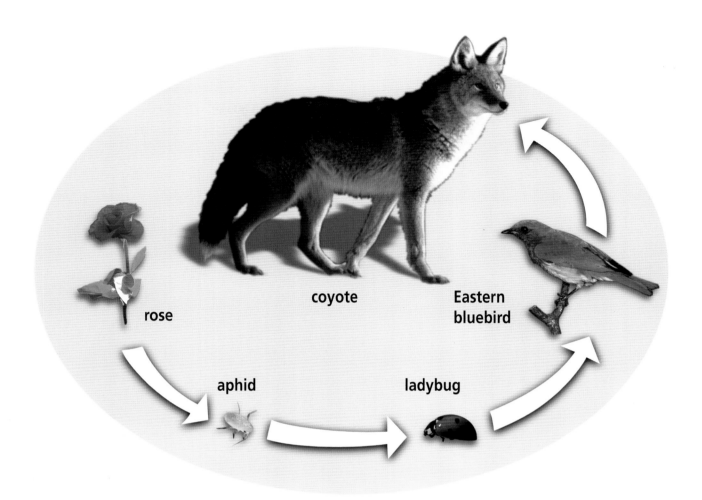

rose

coyote

Eastern
bluebird

aphid

ladybug

One example of a food web starts with a plant. Tiny insects called aphids live on plants and eat the juices from their stems. The aphids are eaten by bigger insects, such as ladybugs. Ladybugs, in turn, may be food for a bird. Many kinds of birds eat insects. Larger animals, such as coyotes, eat birds.

Puzzler

Many people would be happy if insects, especially mosquitoes and flies, disappeared. What would happen if insects really were to disappear?

Answer:
Insects are food for many other animals, including birds and mammals. If there were no insects, many of these animals would starve to death.

Insects for Dinner

Insects are food not only for birds. For example, many people around the world happily eat insects. Insects are often one of the best and easiest forms of food available to people.

In China, some people enjoy eating giant silkworms.

Some people in Africa think termites are a special treat. In some parts of China, people eat cockroaches. Some insects taste like nuts. Others taste like fish. Some are sweet like candy.

Eating insects is not for everyone. Many people and animals enjoy eating food made by insects. Honey is made by honeybees. The bees collect nectar from plants and then mix it with their saliva. Bears like the taste of honey so much they will allow themselves to be stung by the bees to get it.

Beekeepers collect honey from beehives. They wear special clothes so that they will not be stung too many times.

Activity

Taste Test

Try to find two different types of honey. With your eyes closed, taste both. Can you tell the difference between the two?

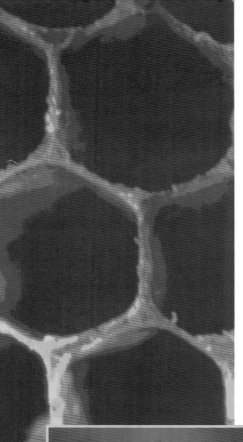

Traveling with the Monarchs

Many insects cannot survive in cold weather. They must find warm homes for winter. Some insects live underground, stay in a nest, or live in our warm houses. Other insects fly to a warmer habitat when winter arrives. This is called migration. Monarch butterflies travel long distances every year. Monarchs live in Canada and the northern United States during the summer. As the weather turns colder, the monarchs head south.

A monarch butterfly may fly as far as 200 miles (320 km) per day! Monarchs fly only during the day when the weather is warm. At night, they rest on trees. Finally, the monarchs reach Mexico. This is where they will spend their winter. The next spring, the monarchs will fly north again.

Hundreds of monarch butterflies fill the air during migration.

Puzzler

Monarch butterflies lay eggs as they fly north in the spring. How do those new butterflies know exactly where to go to spend their spring and winter?

Answer: Scientists are not sure how newly born butterflies know where to go. By the time the eggs hatch into larvae, and complete their development into butterflies, their parents are gone. But each year, they return to exactly the same spots as their parents do.

Ancient Insects

Insects have been around for a long time. Scientists know that many different types of insects lived 300 million years ago. Many of those ancient insects looked like insects we know today. Dragonflies looked just the same — but were much larger.

Fossils tell scientists about these ancient insects. Fewer insect fossils exist than other animal fossils. This is partly because insects have no inner bones. **Fossilized** bones often tell scientists what an animal looked like, or when it lived. Much of what we know about dinosaurs comes from finding fossilized bones and footprints.

Unlike dinosaurs, insects did not leave behind bones. But some fossils of insects can be found in amber. Amber is fossilized tree sap. It looks like a beautiful, clear, yellow stone. Ancient insects got stuck in the tree sap and died. The sap turned into amber over millions of years. Today, those insects can still be seen in amber.

Puzzler

Insects trapped in amber tell us how insects looked millions of years ago. Most of the time, scientists have to guess what an animal looked like. Why?

Answer: Most fossils only show us the bones and footprints of an animal. Scientists have to guess at the shape and color of an animal.

Glossary

adapt: to become suited to a certain environment or way of life by changing gradually over a long period of time.

arachnids: a group of animals, including spiders, that are related to insects.

camouflage: to blend in with the surroundings.

chrysalis: the pupa stage in a butterfly's life cycle.

classify: to arrange animals or plants into groups by comparing their features.

egg: the first stage of an insect's life cycle.

entomologists: people who study insects.

exoskeleton: the hard outer shell of all insects.

fiber: a fine, threadlike substance.

fossilized: to change into a fossil.

fossils: the remains of plants or animals found hardened in layers of rock.

habitat: the environment in which an insect lives.

larva: the wingless stage of an insect's life cycle.

migration: an animal's travels to a new area during different times of the year.

molt: to shed skin and grow.

nectar: a sweet liquid in many flowers.

nymph: a young insect that looks like a small adult.

pollinate: to carry pollen from one flower to another.

pupa: the inactive stage of an insect's life cycle.

reproduction: the joining together of animals to produce young.

species: a group of similar living organisms that only mate with each other.

Index

Web Sites

www.cyberbee.net/bugeat

www.yucky.com/worm

www.entsoc.org/educate.htm

www.naturalpartners.org/InsectZoo

Some web sites stay current longer than others. For further web sites, use your search engines to locate the following topics: *bumblebee*, *butterfly*, *insects*, and *spiders*.